Contents

Introduction: Seasons of the Spirit

ost people have a favourite season. I enjoy living in
a country which has different seasons; would we
enjoy our favourite one as much if it were not for
the contrast? In the name of progress, however, we have lost
something of traditional seasonal living: we can buy fruit
and vegetables at any time of the year, for example. Eating
strawberries in February does not seem right to me and, as a
family who believed that parsnips should not be eaten before the
first frost, they do not seem quite the same in August. Similarly,
flowers that we once associated with certain seasons can now
be purchased at any time of the year in our supermarkets. Yet
despite these developments, with all our knowledge and skills,
we cannot change the weather!

Our purpose here, however, is not to learn how to garden
or grow produce through the different times of the year but
to consider the different spiritual rhythms in our lives. As we
consider the different seasons of life we need to remember that
this is not rooted in one particular biblical passage providing a
type of blueprint for our lives, but the content of each session
reflects the rhythms of life that we see clearly in evidence in
Scripture. Also, we should bear in mind that we are not talking
about different ages – we don't start life in spring and work our
way through to winter as we get older, though it may sometimes
seem like that. As we consider our place spiritually we may move
backwards and forwards through the various seasons, sometimes
visiting all four within a day or so, but other times finding
ourselves in a particular one for some years. It may be helpful to

think of these seasons as rhythms of life that come and go and seem to carry a different heartbeat.

In His teaching, Jesus drew on many everyday features of life, including references to nature's seasons, to illustrate spiritual truths. So it is in His good company that we draw on our everyday experiences of living in the seasons to help us consider where we are on our spiritual journey. The theme also appears in the book of Ecclesiastes, which we will turn to in our concluding chapter.

There is a time for everything,
and a season for every activity under heaven ...
Ecclesiastes 3:1

In most places in the world we will encounter changing climatic seasons, though they are different in type, intensity and timing. Despite concerns over climate change, here in the UK we continue to work our lives around spring, summer, autumn and winter and these will be our focus during these Bible studies, while we acknowledge the different experiences of seasons elsewhere in the world.

This study was given birth some years ago in one of our weekends of spiritual refreshment for women at Waverley, led by Jeannette Barwick and her team with Beverley Shepherd, Beth Clarke and Nicky-Sue Leonard (now Reverend Nicky-Sue Terry). Since then it has been presented as one of our popular regional seminars which we take to different parts of the country, taught by Jeannette and me. My thanks go to those named above who originally worked on this theme which I have been pleased to be able to take forward into the present 'Women at Waverley' programme. I am also grateful to those who have so helpfully contributed to this study guide – to Jeannette Barwick, Beverley Shepherd, Elizabeth Hodkinson, Sharon Prior, Wendy Bray and to my friend Doreen Bairstow, who has been a 'seasoned' traveller with me whilst writing this study guide.

Making the most of the studies

Seasons can be used following attending the seminar or it can be an ideal 'stand alone' as a personal study, on a one to one basis or in a group.

Personal Study

It can be easy to start on such a workbook with great intentions, but some forethought may help you to complete it. Plan a particular time into your week when you can give your full attention to reading and reflecting on each section. If you do not already use a journal you might find it useful to try this helpful way of recording your thoughts both at the time and as you continue to reflect throughout the week.

Group Study

Rather than work on your own, your preference may be to use the workbook in a group setting, in which case there are two possibilities: a weekly group session or possibly a weekend away. Whichever you choose it is useful to have a group leader and also, perhaps, small group co-ordinators for larger groups.

Whilst the workbook is designed to need very little preparation, it is helpful for the leader to be familiar with both the material and the people in the group. The studies will be most effective if people are able to be honest with themselves and with others and so it is important that the leader facilitates in such a way that all the members feel comfortable and secure with each other, knowing that they can rely on the confidentiality of the group and that they are able to be open without fear of being judged. Allowing time for people to share what has impacted them will bring encouragement and opportunities to pray with each other. Encouragement also to take some time to reflect on each session in between meeting will bring added value to both the individuals and to the group as a whole.

If the sessions are going to be the focus of a weekend away, thought will be required as to how they are going to be spread across the days in order to give sufficient time to the different subjects.

Session Format

To enable the smooth running of sessions, each one has been set out in a similar format. However, planning is still necessary; it is useful to become acquainted with the suggested scriptures and to pray for the group study in advance.

Besides introductory reading on the subject being addressed, each session includes a number of small sections: 'Consider' offers discussion about a particular season, 'Study and Discuss' provides the chance to get to know how you honestly think or respond, with the opportunity to discuss together with others, and 'Going Further' involves addressing issues at a more challenging level.

My prayer is that as you use these studies, whether as an individual or as a group, you will be encouraged to see the blessings and the challenges of each of the seasons; to recognise where you may be now and how you might best use this season of life; but also to know that you will not always be there. Remember again that they are not about our age or about the time of year. They are about learning to discern and appreciate what is happening in your life and how to walk with God through all the different rhythms of life. The different stages of life come and go as with the rhythm of the seasonal changes. The questions to ask are: 'Where am I in relation to God at this time?' 'How can I make the most of this stage?' and 'How might I be better prepared for what is to come?'

I encourage you to celebrate what is good in your present season of life.

SESSION 1 –
Winter

Winter

In repentance and rest is your salvation, in quietness and trust is your strength.

Isaiah 30:15

Consider...

What pictures does winter conjure up in your mind?

The coming of winter

We start with winter, a season which we sometimes see as coming at the end of a cycle but equally can be taken as the beginning: our year both starts and ends with winter.

It can be a season with weather we dread, as we are reminded in the carol:

In the bleak midwinter, frosty wind made moan,
Earth stood hard as iron, water like a stone.

However, winter can also be a very positive time. Although the nights begin to draw in and we feel the effects of the weather, there is some solace in returning home from a cold and busy day, drawing the curtains and feeling cosy in front of the fire. Winter is a season of rest. It may not feel like that to us in the weeks leading up to Christmas, but in the natural world it is a time when many plants lie alive but dormant under the soil. As such, it is a vital part of the cycle which will enable the flowering of summer.

Rest is not easy to find in twenty-first-century living. I have a cartoon that amuses me which says 'If I do tomorrow's work today I may get the last day of my life free'. Do you have the tendency to live like that? I know this is true for many people for whom the need to rest feels like a sign of failure. We can become addicted to busyness: it helps us feel good about ourselves, and it may even help us feel that we are that bit better than other people because we are so much busier. I can see this tendency in my own life. But in living like this we are in danger of ignoring an important part of God's original creation design for us: that of rest.

If we find relaxing difficult, this needs to be confronted. We need to recognise that our worth is not based on how many activities we are involved in within our church or community, or how many extra hours we put into our work. Our value is not based on how hard we work but on how God sees us. I believe it was Martin Luther who said:

God does not love us because we are valuable. We are valuable because God loves us.

Sabbath rest

Rest is an important principle to incorporate into our lives because it is a very clear biblical principle. It could be called Sabbath rest and to unpack that, we need to go back to the beginning of the Bible.

Read and consider the following passages.

Genesis 2:1–3

We see in these verses how God models to us the rhythm of work and rest. In this account of creation what did God do on the seventh day? He rested! And did the newly created world grind to a halt as a result? If it is good enough for God to rest then I think it is good enough for you and me to rest too. Max Lucado writes, 'God's message is plain, "If creation didn't crash when I rested, it won't crash when you do."'[1]

Exodus 20:8–11

Here we see that God did not suggest rest as an occasional reward, He actually commands it! Note how much space and detail is given to this one commandment. I wonder how many of us have asked for forgiveness when we have broken one of the other commandments yet easily ignore this one. When was the last time you asked for forgiveness for not resting?! We read how God blessed the Sabbath day as a day of rest. And how many of us fail to receive this particular blessing, not because God has withheld it but simply because we are too tired to receive anything? God knows our need to rest because it was part of His design plan for us: we would do well to welcome it.

Mark 2:27

On this occasion, Jesus reaffirms the Sabbath rest principle, pointing out that the Sabbath was made as a day of rest for our benefit and not as something that was to be burdensome.

Active resting

Resting can sometimes be interpreted as laziness or simply 'taking it easy', but there is more than that to *active* rest.

Sometimes we need to stop 'doing' in order to take time to meet with God. This is a time when we can refocus; when we 'clear the decks' in order to gain a clearer godly perspective on things. It is a time when we put down our roots deeply into God.

Some years ago, I was in a time of spiritual winter which I had not welcomed. I was feeling dry and without a lot of life. I happened to be at a training day at Waverley when Nigel James, then counselling training coordinator, spoke about a time when he visited a vineyard in Samos, Cyprus. Fire had destroyed more than 30 per cent of the island's vegetation three years previously, yet amazingly, shoots had begun to emerge. The vineyard owner explained that vines have exceptionally strong and long taproots which penetrate deep through the rocky, dry soil in search of sustenance and water. It was such a timely reminder to me that even when we seem to be in barren and difficult times, if we are deeply rooted in God then we can have the confidence that we still have life and that we will recover and flourish once again.

In nature's winter the activity may not be seen above the ground but it is continuing below. So in our spiritual winter, even though little seems to be happening on the surface, much could be going on below.

Winter, then, is a time

to **stop**

to **listen**

to **refocus**

to **ask**: Where have I been putting my energies? Have I been focusing on the important rather than just the urgent? What does God want for me now – what is His next step for me?

to **prepare** for this next season.

I once had a period of time when I seemed to have reached a crossroads: a particular role had come to an end. It felt very strange and my first instinct was to rush out and find the next thing that I should do. But I believed I should wait and, though it seemed uncomfortable at first, it became a very special time for me. Through it God taught me a great deal, but I needed first to stop in order to listen and get clarity. I am hanging on to those lessons now. This year has been overwhelmingly busy at times, and it has been hard to stop and give up a complete day to listening to God, but I have learned that *not* to do so is not really an option.

At the start of the year (January 2009), I made a commitment that I would take one day out each month and spend it with God in whatever way seemed most appropriate. I decided that whenever possible I would spend that time at a local Christian centre which offers quiet days. January came and went, and I did not make it – I simply did not 'have time'! February came; I gritted my teeth, booked the day and fell asleep on the chapel floor!

In March, I put off the phone call to book the day until the last moment. Yet both of those occasions became special as I simply spent time with God. They were days that enabled me to do the work of 'summer' with a God-centred focus.

Enforced rest

Rest sounds an inviting word. However, our personal winter may not be such a positive time. Remember the words of 'In the Bleak Midwinter'? Winter is a cold time of year in the UK. It can be harsh and bleak and this can bring loneliness to those unable to get out and about. Just as winter is a time of physical coldness, our personal 'winter' may be marked by emotional coldness, perhaps accompanied by hurt and rejection. We may feel as though we are alone; that friends have abandoned us and that even God is absent.

It is at such times we need to know that this is a passing season and that God is with us, that He will never leave or abandon us.

At some time in our lives we will all face enforced rest. It may be personal illness, or that of a family member, bereavement, redundancy, depression or a change of location. These all impact our lives. We may welcome or fight against such imposed changes to our normal lifestyle.

• •

Some years ago Jeannette Barwick, the founder of the women's ministry at Waverley Abbey House, experienced enforced rest. She learned that this season can be seen as God's gift to us. She writes:

Our spiritual winters may be chosen or enforced. Sometimes we encounter different life circumstances that thrust us into the season of winter. Illness, for instance, may be one way we experience enforced rest. In the year I was 60, I was diagnosed with cancer of the colon. I had to have major surgery and seven

months of chemotherapy. I made a good recovery and I thank
God for restoring me so thoroughly, but I had to go through that
experience.

The discovery came at a time when I was in the midst of a
very busy programme and so I was suddenly plucked out of
my schedule of activity. However, none of us is indispensible,
whatever we might think, and others were able to take up my
appointments.

God gave me rest in that winter experience and used
two special channels in particular to minister His peace and
encouragement into my heart. The first was the people of God
– from all around the world and my own family – who expressed
to me their love and prayerful concern in many ways and were
quite marvellous in their support.

The other was a lovely visual aid from the world of nature.
When they heard of my diagnosis, my friends at *Woman Alive*
magazine sent me this scripture from Ruth 2:12: 'May the Lord
repay you for what you have done. May you be richly rewarded
by the LORD, the God of Israel, under whose wings you have
come to take refuge.' I happen to live overlooking a river and
sometimes the river birds nest beneath my kitchen window.
The very weekend I was told I had cancer, two swans began
to build a large nest. Over the weeks of my convalescence I
watched a beautiful example played out on the river bank as to
what it means to take refuge under the wings of the Almighty.
I saw the swans take it in turns to sit on the nest, their huge
wings keeping the eggs – and later the cygnets – sheltered and
protected. Soon the tiny cygnets were in the water learning to
paddle. One day I even saw a tiny one being carried along on its
mother's back, nestling between her huge wings. That scripture
and the image of nestling under His wings brought home to me

the reality of God's overshadowing presence. I felt calm and relaxed as the truth became a reality to me, reinforced by what was happening day by day, week by week and month by month under my kitchen window.

God used that experience not just to restore me to physical health but to touch every other area of my life as well. He wonderfully strengthened and refreshed me spiritually and emotionally too. How I thank and praise Him for His intimate care and love and for the deeper relationship with Him that ensued. How tenderly the Lord deals with us as we face difficulties in our lives. The principles I learned then have helped to sustain me in other spiritual winters since.

•••

 Study and discuss

1. **Read Exodus 20:1–18.** Re-read the commandment in verses 8–10.
Why do you think this was included and why in such detail?

What was your initial response to reading this? How do you now respond to the fact that taking rest is one of the Ten Commandments? Do you find this commandment easy or difficult to follow?

How do you go about keeping this commandment?

What are the obstacles that get in the way of you taking this rest? What are the consequences of choosing not to rest?

2. Read Mark 6:7–13,30,31. What did Jesus invite the disciples to do at the end of their busy and successful preaching tour? Take that phrase in verse 31, "'Come with me by yourselves to a quiet place and get some rest'". Hear it as if from Jesus to you.

3. When did you last face an unwelcome personal winter? Can you identify what helped you get through it?

4. Looking back to other winter experiences, what good things came out of them?

5. If you are reading this in winter, take a walk outside; if it is another time of year, close your eyes and take an imaginary winter walk. What do you see around you? Let God's creation speak to you about parallels between this physical season and what might be going on in your own life at this time.
What might be (a) comforting, and (b) challenging for you as you ponder on these parallels?

This is a season that we may see as a regular daily, weekly or monthly rhythm in our personal lives. Sometimes it goes on for a much longer period. We can choose to fight it, be fearful of it, or to see it as God's gift to us: a time to regain our bearings and perspective, a time to develop deeper intimacy with God.

Spring and summer will come, but we can only make the most of the opportunities of those seasons if we have taken the time to develop our relationship with God. We can therefore see winter as a friend – a time of renewal and strengthening – as we open ourselves to the work of the Holy Spirit in our lives.

 ## Going further

1. Read and study the following passages.

Isaiah 30:15 Israel had failed to trust in God and chose to turn to Egypt. God challenges the nation and points to the need to actively turn back to God. In place of a restless anxiety and rushing to resolve the situation in what seems the best way to them, the people of God should instead rest in the Lord with a sense of purposeful trust.

As you meditate on this verse ask God what He wants to say to you. What is your Egypt? Where do you rush to in order to resolve your problems?

Matthew 11:28–30 Look this up in different translations of the Bible if possible. **Do you feel burdened by the demands of work, family, Christians, the church, God? What might you be able to do to achieve a good balance if you do not already have it?**

Mark 6:30–31 Picture yourself in this scene. How do you react and respond to the words of Jesus?

Prayer

Father, help me to welcome those winter times when I can stop and take time just 'to be' and to develop a deeper relationship with You and develop a greater trust in you.

Into Your hands, Father God, Jesus Christ, Holy Spirit I commit my life, my work, my relationships, myself. Amen.

Note

1. Max Lucado, *Traveling Light* (Nashville, TN: Thomas Nelson, 2001) p.42.

SESSION 2 –
Spring

Spring

See! The winter is past;
the rains are over and gone.
Flowers appear on the earth;
the season of singing has come ...

Song of Songs 2:11–12

Consider...

What is it about spring that you enjoy?

Are there any things associated with springtime which you do not like?

The joys of spring

Springtime is associated with new beginnings; a time for new growth. We look forward to the lighter mornings and evenings and to the summer months ahead. It is a time for future plans but also of present activity as we get out into our gardens and start planting and getting them ready for their busiest time; we enjoy watching those shoots push through the ground and colour coming to the trees. It has also traditionally been the time for spring cleaning, again getting ready for the months to come.

And so it is in our spiritual lives that we have those seasons where we sense something is going to change, something new is emerging and it is with feelings of excitement, anticipation and, perhaps, with some trepidation that we get ready.

When were you last aware of those stirrings inside? Or maybe you feel those stirrings right now.

Potential difficulties of personal springtime

Imagine yourself feeling a growing anticipation or excitement about what may lie ahead. You start to see possibilities as more, rather than less, likely to happen. But then someone *bursts the bubble*. It may be your spouse, your church leader, your employer or a friend. The message they give is that you are not being realistic; you don't have the time, the qualifications, the skills, the resources. This can create tension as you struggle with these people who differ from you in their vision and in seeing the possibilities. It might even be that these negative messages are coming from within yourself as you tussle with the potential but lack confidence in yourself. You are not the first, and are not alone in your doubts. I too, along with many others, have been there.

Many Christians in such situations have taken courage from Joshua:

> 'Be strong and very courageous. Be careful to obey all the
> law my servant Moses gave you; do not turn from it to the
> right or to the left, that you may be successful wherever you
> go. Do not let this Book of the Law depart from your mouth;
> meditate on it day and night, so that you may be careful
> to do everything written in it. Then you will be prosperous
> and successful. Have I not commanded you? Be strong and
> courageous. Do not be terrified; do not be discouraged, for
> the LORD your God will be with you wherever you go.'
>
> *Joshua 1:7–9*

Elizabeth Hodkinson, the Director of Training at Waverley, writes about Mary, the mother of Jesus. Mary is a remarkable example of someone who was faced with life-changing circumstances to which she had to respond.

Mary – a model (Luke 1:26–56)

Obviously, Mary is unique, and God's plan for her was unique. But so is His plan for each one of us. The important thing is to be open to those plans, and Mary is a wonderful model here. God's word to her sounded completely impossible, but 'nothing is impossible with God', as the angel Gabriel told her. In one way

31

her life wouldn't be different to the usual: marriage, children, widowhood, but in reality it would be extraordinary and life-changing for humanity. So might our lives be too.

Are you open to God's plan for your life, whatever new season He brings? Are you ready to hear His word to you today? Will you be part of *His* plan, rather than asking Him to bless *your* plans?

Just look at God's plan for Mary. She's to have a baby, miraculously, and He is to be the Son of God! That's from God's perspective. But from the Nazareth perspective, this respectable young Jewish girl will face shame, misunderstanding and gossip. What will her parents say? What will Joseph say? This will take Mary way out of her comfort zone.

Are we, too, prepared to go out of our comfort zone? Would we like to be prepared? If so, Mary offers us a response: 'I am the Lord's servant … let it be to me as you have said' (Luke 1:38).

The angel departs. Left behind is a shaken young girl with a literally incredible story to tell her parents – but with one startling fact that can be corroborated. According to Gabriel, Elizabeth, her elderly relative, is six months pregnant. She is way down south in Judah, and Mary is in Nazareth, but we read that Mary 'got ready and hurried to a town in the hill country of Judea' (Luke 1:39). Just a small sentence, but it represents an enormous journey. How does a young girl go that distance?

As I see it, Mary is now not only out of her comfort zone, but pressing against all the cultural norms of her day. A young girl, low down in the family pecking order, at the centre of attention and insisting on going to see Elizabeth. But go she does. I imagine her arriving at Elizabeth's and calling out her greeting. Is she full of faith, or feeling foolish and uncertain? Will she find a blossoming mother-to-be, or just a slim, elderly woman with sadness in her eyes?

Mary's feelings don't actually matter. She's come, and that is the point. And she finds Elizabeth heavily pregnant and radiant, filled with the Holy Spirit, and confirming Mary's own pregnancy, as yet invisible. Not just the pregnancy, but its extraordinary nature: 'The mother of my Lord', Elizabeth declares (Luke 1:43). Stimulated by that wonderful prophecy, Mary herself prophesies, placing her own story in God's big story – alongside Abraham, Israel, and the future generations of God's people.

Think what Mary would have missed if she'd stayed at home. But she went, found encouragement, and was stimulated to greater faith. Is there something that you should be doing in follow-up to a word from the Lord? Perhaps something that requires you to step out in faith, perhaps against the surrounding cultural pressures and expectations? Take Mary as a model, and go for it!

A spiritual spring clean

So how can we be getting ready for our spiritual summer whilst also enjoying the present spring? As I look back on the various new paths I have taken I am reminded of the ways I have prepared for what is to come.

• Find suitable training. Following my most recent extended 'winter experiences' I knew it was time to move onwards and decided that my next move was to apply for the Certificate in Christian Counselling at Waverley. This equipped me wonderfully for the plans God had for me. For you, it may be a day, evening, weekend, week-long or even longer course that will equip you better. Maybe it is learning to drive, attending a creative writing course or art class, or preparing for active service in retirement. Or it may be about getting ready for marriage or childbirth with marriage preparation or parenting classes to consider.

• Read. Scour your local library, bookshops, friends' and minister's bookshelves for relevant books and magazine articles.

• Talk to people who know you. Listen to advice from wise people who can see your gifts and potential. If you feel a calling to some activity within your church discuss it with your church leaders so that you remain within the authority structure of the church.

• Spend time with people who are faith-builders and avoid people who will be discouraging. It is good to get advice from people who are realistic and can spot difficulties for you, but if something inside you has ignited a passion, take care to nurture it by being in the company of those who can share and encourage your vision.

• Research and explore. When I first felt drawn to leading women's conferences in my area of Dorset I got as much information as possible; finding out what was already available, what other churches were doing, and how other people advertised.

• Spend time with God. Although last on this list, it needs to be central to any plan of action for all seasons, not just for spring. It may be setting aside time to go on retreat, or just retreating with God while at home. Walking, driving, swimming or other activities where you are able to quieten your voice in order to hear His voice can be useful times when used intentionally. Remember that *listening to* God is more effective than *talking at* Him. You may hear God through everyday circumstances; by reading books, through music, in a sermon, through the comments and advice of people you trust, through creation and so many other ways.

One important way of hearing from God is by reading His word – the Bible. As we read Scripture so God can speak through it to our situations.

Your word is a lamp to my feet and a light for my path.
Psalm 119:105

When the writers of the psalms were referring to the word or words of God, they were not thinking of the Bible. The Old Testament did not exist as such and the New Testament accounts had yet to happen. However, Christians since the Early Church have believed that the Bible, although written by many individuals, contains God's words to us. And so we are in agreement with the psalmist when he writes, 'Your word is a light for my feet', when we acknowledge that we can discover ways in which God is guiding us through reading Scripture, and allowing His principles and priorities to take central place in our lives.

Study and discuss

1. Can you remember a time when you were considering something new in your life; a new job or role within your work, a new area of church or community service, or a change in family circumstances?
Make a list of the emotions you felt, dividing them into positive and negative feelings. How did you deal with these emotions at the time?

2. Read Joshua chapter 1.
Note one phrase that is repeated four times. Why is repetition important?

Joshua was given reasons for having confidence in God. What were they? What gives you strength and confidence?

Read through the passage again and note down phrases that you can hold on to as your treasured phrases of Scripture.

3. Read Luke 1:26–56. Look again at the character of Mary. It may be that any new things approaching for you will not rock any boats, but it may be, like Mary, you recognise that you will be taken out of your comfort zone and even face negative responses from people.
If this is true for you, what are the implications and what might you learn from Mary about how to handle them?

Look back to how you answered the questions in *Consider...* at the beginning of this section. What personal and spiritual parallels can you draw?

 Going further

1. Take one of the verses below. Read the verse through slowly. Re-read it, taking a word or short phrase at a time. Chew over each word or phrase. Then look at the verse again and meditate on it as a whole verse.

> *I wait for the LORD, my soul waits, and in his word I put my hope.*
>
> *Psalm 130:5*

> *Your word is a lamp to my feet and a light for my path.*
>
> *Psalm 119:105*

2. Read Isaiah 30:15.

> *In **repentance** and **rest** is your **salvation**, in **quietness** and **trust** is your **strength**.*

This verse has been used in both winter and spring chapters of this book. Take each word that has been highlighted and ask God to speak to you through each of them. Then take the phrase as a whole and pray these words into your life. If you sense that there is something new on the horizon, draw up your plan of action.

Hearing through Scripture

It is good to vary the way we read the Bible. Sometimes reading a complete book in one sitting, for example a New Testament letter, can be helpful. Other times it is better to concentrate on smaller segments, or even a phrase or word. When it comes to biblical meditation, I like the picture of a cow chewing the cud. The cow gets all the goodness out of the food which then goes into its stomach. However, that is not the end of it as the semi digested food, the cud, returns from the stomach to the mouth to be chewed a second and third time. This way the cow can extract the very best out of every mouthful.

Just as the idiomatic expression 'chewing the cud' means meditating or pondering, over a prolonged period, to meditate on a passage of Scripture requires time to read and reread, to get as much out of it as possible and then to go back for more!

Prayer

Heavenly Father, thank You for the delights of spring and the joy of new beginnings. May Your Word continue to inspire, instruct and guide me as I seek to look to You for the way ahead. May I take courage and confidence from the knowledge that You will equip me for whatever task You call me to do.

Into Your hands, Father God, Jesus Christ, Holy Spirit I commit my life, my work, my relationships, myself. Amen.

SESSION 3 –
Summer

Summer

But the fruit of the Spirit is love, joy, peace, patience, kindness, goodness, faithfulness, gentleness and self-control.

Galatians 5:22–23

Consider...

Think about last summer. What did you most enjoy?

What do you least like about summer?

Salad days!

Summer – what is it about summer that brings a tingle? Maybe you prefer one of the other seasons but summer is probably the one enjoyed most. I'm not sure how true it has been of recent years but summer brings to my mind childhood holidays, days out, picnics, barbecues, the warmth of the sun, and those bright mornings and warm evenings.

Summer is nature's season of abundance and fruitfulness. Living in an area awash with 'pick your own' farms and growing a few of our own vegetables it is noticeable that much of our produce grows best at this time of year; summer is a prolific time for farmers and home gardeners alike.

Spiritual summer

Just as summer is a time for nature's fruitfulness, so our spiritual summer is a season where we look for spiritual fruitfulness. We have spent time planning and preparing as we considered in the previous study and now it is time to reap the benefits of spring; it is time to grow and go!

WHAT TYPE OF FRUIT DO WE HOPE FOR?

IN OUR CHARACTER

We usually think of spiritual fruit as the result of *what we do*, but I want to start with the recognition that it is also about *who we are* which lays the foundation for the other aspects of fruitfulness.

The apostle Paul speaks of the fruit of the Spirit as being love, joy, peace, patience, kindness, goodness, faithfulness, gentleness and self control (Gal. 5:22–23). Just as the thought of summer brings a smile to many faces, I think that something similar happens when we encounter people who clearly demonstrate these characteristics: they bring a warmth and pleasure to others as they convey something of the Spirit of God in their lives.

However, I suggest that we need some of the experiences of winter and spring before we can really live this out. It is only when we have experienced the more difficult times that we can show deep and genuine patience and faithfulness. These characteristics often emerge from times of personal suffering which increase our personal understanding of the needs of others. How aware are you of this type of fruitfulness in your life?

IN OUR WORK

Even though we may not always see it ourselves, work, whether it is paid or unpaid, in the home or in secular employment, will be enhanced when we work with our heart in it. To see the results of our labour and energy is a reward in itself and a source of great joy and satisfaction.

Sometimes we see the fruit – I have wonderful experiences of bumping into people who have been to Waverley or who I know from my time at Moorlands College who surprise me by sharing how something I said or did helped them. That is encouraging. But I know very little, if anything, about the difference I made to the lives of the children I taught at secondary school, or my former teaching colleagues, or those in the toddler groups I helped lead. I cannot say I saw any 'ripened fruit' at the time, but I passionately believe that those contacts were every bit as important in the kingdom of God equation.

IN OUR COMMUNITIES

Jesus said that His followers are the salt of the earth (Matt. 5:13). If that is true for us then we will have an impact for good in the smaller communities of our homes, in the wider communities of our churches and neighbourhoods and even further afield with people we might never even meet. I think back to people who have had an impact on my life – a young student preacher, a pastor's wife, an artist, a singer, a flower arranger, a friend. God has used each of these, amongst many others, to help me grow. How many people have influenced me – yet they never knew it? That knowledge encourages me to believe that you and I will have 'fruit' that we have no idea about, and, though much of it may come about in our spiritual summer, good also comes at other times, when we might be least expecting it.

And so as we recognise growth and development in our inner lives which then impacts our outer lives, we understand more clearly that our lives have purpose and meaning. We see we can make a difference, and that is rewarding whether that change is for just one or two people or for crowds. I encourage you to celebrate the signs of summer in your life, both past and present.

The source of our spiritual fruitfulness

'I am the true vine, and my Father is the gardener. He cuts off every branch in me that bears no fruit, while every branch that does bear fruit he prunes so that it will be even more fruitful. You are already clean because of the word I have spoken to you. Remain in me, as I also remain in you. No branch can bear fruit by itself; it must remain in the vine. Neither can you bear fruit unless you remain in me. I am the vine; you are the branches. If you remain in me and I in you, you will bear much fruit; apart from me you can do nothing.'

John 15:1–5

It is as we remain close to Jesus, as we listen to His voice, as we read His words in the Gospels, as we determine to follow His lead, that we can truly find fruitfulness. The branch that draws constantly from the main part of the vine is going to bear grapes. If we are constantly drawing on Jesus' life-giving presence then we are in a good place to bear spiritual fruit.

Summer madness

It's not all good, however. Living in a popular holiday area, I am also aware of the general busyness that comes with summer and holidaymakers, especially on the roads. When we get a good summer there are always those who suffer from too much sunshine. At other times, there are those disappointed holidaymakers wandering forlornly around our seaside towns in the rain, having come with hopes of sunny days on the beach.

Other problems beset the gardener in summer. How often

have you come home from holiday to a tangled wilderness with dry, brown lawns? We know that, though we might enjoy the seasonal colour and produce, summer also brings a very heavy workload as we struggle to keep the weeds down and ensure that the ground is watered enough.

And so it is with our spiritual summer; there are some aspects we need to be wary of. We need to remember that whilst the buzz and activity of 'summer' brings life and energy, for some it can be wearing. We may extend ourselves too much or we might be disappointed when all our work seems to go unnoticed or unappreciated by others. Similarly, in spiritual summer time, with all its frenetic activity, it is all too easy to get caught up in the busyness of all that we are involved in so that we forget to stop to replenish and refresh ourselves. Just as we need water in the summer more than any other time, we need to be constantly drawing from the 'fount of living water' when we are being spiritually fruitful, and be certain that we place our dependency on God, otherwise we will not survive the heat. Tony Horsfall writes:

'Perhaps in our activity-dominated lives, we have forgotten what it is to linger in the presence of Jesus. Perhaps, in our desire to achieve external goals, we have neglected the development of our inner life – less measurable, but much more vital ... It takes time to abide in Christ ...'[1]

• •

Beverley Shepherd writes about a dream she had where it was evident that God wanted to draw her attention to the dangers of such 'summer madness'.

The dream concerned a rail journey. I was travelling by train to a large city, arriving at one terminus and then needing to continue my journey from a second terminus some way across the city. Bicycles were provided to cross the city, but I only had three minutes to make my connection. I pedalled furiously whilst clutching a parcel containing something very precious. Worn out, I arrived at the second terminus with time to spare, but had lost the parcel! Still, with my thirty remaining seconds I could retrace my journey and find it – or so I thought. The precious parcel had disappeared and in its place I collected several other parcels – all jiffy bags full of bubble wrap. I dashed back to the second terminus and leapt onto the train as it was pulling out of the station. Making my way to a corner seat I collapsed, absolutely exhausted, and surrounded by my parcels full of nothing. It was then that I awoke.

I knew the dream had been a warning – 'What was in that first parcel that was so precious?' was my anxious question as I prayed. God showed me. I picked up my diary and started to rearrange my schedule. My diary is not that easy to reorganise, with many events being booked several months in advance. Six months later the changes started to bear fruit and I realised with both shock and gratitude that God's warning had come just in time.[2]

Another area we need to be aware of in this season is potential pride which, like a veracious garden weed, can spoil and overcome the good. As we see fruit from our work we may consider it the result of our own efforts alone. I feel blessed when I see people who I have been able to help on their journey, but I need to remember that this is God's work not mine.

You may say to yourself, 'My power and the strength of my hands have produced this wealth for me.' But remember the LORD your God, for it is he who gives you the ability to produce wealth ...

Deuteronomy 8:17–18

Other such 'weeds' might be conceit and envy, which Paul warns us about:

Since we live by the Spirit, let us keep in step with the Spirit. Let us not become conceited, provoking and envying each other.

Galatians 5:26

We can enjoy satisfaction in knowing we have helped others but we need to remember that it is God's work, whether it is people who come to faith, people who have been helped to move further along in their Christian lives, or those we have encouraged in some way.

 Study and discuss:

1. Read Galatians 5:22–26.
What 'fruit' are you aware of in your life, work and community? Where would you like to see more 'fruit'?

2. Read John 15:1–5 and 16.
Take some time to meditate on verse 16 and write down any thoughts that come to you.

3. How do you feel about the spiritual season of summer?

4. Make a list of up to ten people who have helped you most in your spiritual life. Write a note of thanks and encouragement to these where possible.

5. Good fruit depends on the preparation of winter and the growth of spring.
What aspects of your spiritual winters and springs have prepared you for spiritual summers you have experienced?

6. What spiritual weeds (the things that could spoil or even strangle the good that you achieve) are you aware of in your life? How might you tackle them?

 Going further

1. Read Ephesians 2:10. Do you recognise and acknowledge those things with which God has gifted you? Are you able to take pleasure in them (which is different from feeling pride)? Have there been times when you have gone ahead with what could be described as 'good works' while aware that they have been *your* plans and not *God's* plans? Are there lessons you can draw from those times? Consider what this verse means for you.

2. Do you ask God to bless your work as a regular prayer? You might find Psalm 90:17 a helpful prayer as you consider your work whenever and whatever it may be:

May the favour of the Lord our God rest upon us;
establish the work of our hands for us –
yes, establish the work of our hands.

Prayer

Father, I surrender all I am and all I do to You. Thank You for the gifts You have given me and I pray for the right opportunities to use them. May I know a deepening of the work of the Holy Spirit in my life with a greater presence of joy, peace, patience, kindness gentleness and self control as I seek to relate to others. And I pray that You will establish the work of my hands.

Into Your hands, Father God, Jesus Christ, Holy Spirit I commit my life, my work, my relationships, myself. Amen.

Notes

1. Tony Horsfall, *A Fruitful Life* (BRF, 2006) p.73.

2. Beverley Shepherd in Jeannette Barwick and Beverley Shepherd, *Seasons of the Spirit* (Farnham: CWR, 2004) pp.22–23.

SESSION 4 –
Autumn

Autumn

'I tell you the truth, unless a grain of wheat falls to the ground and dies, it remains only a single seed. But if it dies, it produces many seeds.'

John 12:24

Consider...

What pictures does autumn create in your mind?

What do you welcome and what do you dread about this time of year?

The colours of autumn

Autumn – a season of sensational change. We watch as the trees give us a dazzling display of colour before their leaves wither and finally fall; crops are harvested and fields replanted, and animals fatten up before the harder months arrive. Before the days of household freezers, autumn was a time to turn to the surplus garden produce and either store carefully, bottle or pickle it for use over the winter months.

Harvesting

It must be a huge relief and great joy to see barns replete with the fruit of months of labour; the culmination of the previous seasons of hard work for the farmer. We also experience joy when we see the effects of spiritual fruit in our lives. This may come as a result of recognising the impact of living in a more godly, Spirit-filled way; it may be seeing people we have influenced for the good, people we have helped find their way into relationship with Christ; it may be groups that we have pioneered or helped to work well.

However, it is possible to be so fearful of pride that we are uncomfortable with recognising the good in ourselves. If that is so, we need to recognise that acknowledging God's work of grace in our lives is honouring to Him. Whether we look back over a day's achievement, a month, a year or a lifetime, let us be ready to enjoy our own equivalent to nature's harvest whilst also thanking God – for ultimately it all comes from Him.

Pause for a moment to reflect on your spiritual harvest and to give thanks to God.

Falling leaves: Relinquishing

Just as in nature's autumn we see the leaves become vibrant and then fade and fall, so at many stages in our lives those things we have enjoyed and done well come to an end.

At times this is welcome change. We feel the moment has come to take a back seat – to let someone else take the reins so that we can enjoy a well-earned rest, or it may be with a sense of anticipation that we end something to make room for a new job or role. We are then ready to start the process of handing over and look forward to it. At other times, however, the thought of relinquishing something that may have been very precious to us and given purpose to our lives may be something we dread. This phase of life can bring anxiety or feelings of dismay. If this is the case, how can we welcome and better use autumn as a positive season in our lives?

Colourful living

I had just started pondering on this chapter when the BBC produced a special autumn edition of *Countryfile* which I found very inspirational. I learned that during autumn, chlorophyll in the leaves is withdrawn; this is what causes the usual green colour to change to browns and reds. Those colours have always been there but just masked by the dominant green.

From this picture of the withdrawal of chlorophyll, several things struck me. First that sometimes we have to lay down one part of us, maybe a role, in order for those other things that are latent within us to rise to the surface. If we never move on we may well miss the joy of a future adventure. Equally, it may be necessary for us to withdraw in order for others to come to the fore, especially when we have been in leadership positions, so that the 'true colours' of others can be recognised and appreciated as they are encouraged to take on new roles. Most importantly, it is as we rein ourselves back that God can come fully into focus in our lives.

We need to recognise that everything has its season and that change need not be feared and may even bring good things. What joy there is in seeing those beautiful colours emerge!

I think of my recent experience in taking on my present role for CWR. It was an exciting prospect but meant laying down other things that I enjoyed – counselling with a local practice, helping with a toddler group, and many of the church activities with which I was involved. I found it hard to stand back from these things but knew it was necessary if I was to function well in my job as a CWR tutor. Not only for me; it was also necessary for those various groups with which I had been working. Whilst maintaining my interest, it was better for them that I withdrew so that they were able to continue more effectively.

In some situations there can be a danger in considering a new role to be of lesser significance; but is it truly a godly perspective to underrate some roles? I look back to the time I gave up my job as a secondary school teacher to be a mother – 'just a mum' as I thought back then. I later realised that my sense of self-worth came through my career rather than from God's estimation of my worth and that to be a mum was an equally high calling.

Read John 3:22–35. John the Baptist recognised the greater authority of Jesus and acknowledged that he needed to stand back in order to let Jesus take His correct place (John 3:30). If we continue to insist on taking centre stage in our lives, we are denying Jesus His rightful place.

Dying to live!

Read John 12:23–26. When we struggle with relinquishing a task or role, it may be wise to examine our motives and priorities. Do we want to retain our independence or are we willing to submit to Christ's lordship in our lives? Jesus' teaching in John's Gospel brings this clearly to our minds and can appear quite disturbing when first read.

> *I tell you the truth, unless a grain of wheat falls to the ground and dies, it remains only a single seed. But if it dies, it produces many seeds. The man who loves his life will lose it, while the man who hates his life in this world will keep it for eternal life.*
>
> *John 12:24–25*

In this analogy to the natural world, the grain of wheat is of no value unless it is buried in the ground. Jesus seems to be saying that in some way, real life requires a death. Ultimately this was true: through His own sacrificial death many have come to experience life. However, this is not a suggestion that we should go out and literally lay down our lives.

And what does it mean to *hate* one's life? Jesus did not mean that we should literally hate ourselves; indeed elsewhere He said that we should love others as we love ourselves, suggesting that loving ourselves is quite appropriate. This phrase draws on a typical way of speaking at the time which expresses two contrasting positions by extreme exaggeration. In other words, the eternal life we are offered is so immensely good that to hold on to our selfish way of living is worthless, or to be 'hated'.

To me this says that if we love ourselves in such a way that we hang on to everything we have and are, we will end up being the poorer. But if we are prepared to lay down our self-centredness, putting God into the central place in our lives and looking to please and follow Him as our first priority, then we can truly flourish. As we serve and allow others to come to the fore, we truly blossom as we also discover the joy of encouraging others.

Falling leaves: Reinvesting

I also discovered from *Countryfile* that trees are adapting to the shorter, colder days by losing their leaves. Without the leaves, the trees can take back the stored sugars, energy and useful products from their extremities in order to help the trunk and roots as they prepare for the next season. This way of giving back this goodness is integral to the continued existence of the tree. What lessons are there for us here?

Our spiritual autumn is a time when we not only enjoy the harvest but also put our wealth of experience and knowledge to good use. I hold to the idea that nothing is wasted in the economy of God, yet how often have I thought that my skills and life experiences were to be wasted because of life's changing circumstances? Later I find that God channels them skilfully into the next part of my life and gives opportunities to invest those skills and experiences in other people. Just as that goodness is reabsorbed back into the tree, allowing it to continue to thrive for future years, so we put back something into the Body of Christ which enables it to continue flourishing.

These days we often use the terms 'mentoring' or 'life-coaching' to describe such activity, but despite such formal sounding titles these are things that we all do at all stages of life, whether as parents, grandparents, youth leaders or even simply as good friends.

· ·

Sharon Prior of Catalyst Training is a freelance trainer, coach and mentor. She writes:

Peggy was seventy-two years old, and had served God faithfully throughout her life. She knew a young woman in her church was thinking about going to Bible college, so invited her for coffee. For four years, until she died, she wrote letters and spoke to the young woman regularly, encouraging her in her faith and helping her with things that she didn't understand as a new Christian. She challenged and inspired her in a very quiet and unassuming way. Nobody knew of Peggy's ministry to this young woman;
it was 'behind the scenes'.
The young woman went into youth work with a Christian organisation after leaving Bible college and she started to do the same thing with the young people she came to know. She walked alongside them, encouraged them into leadership and helped them develop their skills to serve God and His kingdom: Peggy's example of investing in young people was carried through to the next generation. In time, the young woman was excited herself as she saw young people taking over the leadership of activities that she had led in the past. She saw young people passing on the baton to those younger than them. Having regularly invested time in two seventeen-year-old girls they, in turn, mentored a ten- and an eight -year-old.
Peggy could have just sat in church each week as she

lived out her days of retirement, but she chose not to, and this resulted in many lives being touched and transformed. This was her ministry of investment, not in the monetary sense, but in lives, which is so much more important.

You wouldn't have heard of Peggy if you hadn't read this story. I know about her because I was the young woman she invited to tea all those years ago. I can honestly say that I would not be the woman I am today if it had not been for Peggy.

So, no matter how old or young you may be, you could be a Peggy to someone in your church. You may not get any human recognition for doing it. But just as leaves fall from the tree and provide nourishment for the new life to come, so, as you mentor another person in the way that Peggy mentored me, you are breathing new life into the Church for the future. What an awesome calling and legacy!

• •

As we read Scripture we find so many examples of men and women who invested in others. For some this came at the end of their lives as they were looking to pass on the baton. For others it happened along the way as they recognised the need to encourage and nurture other people.

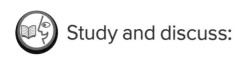 Study and discuss:

1. Read Deuteronomy 31:1,2,7–9,14 and 34:1–9. Moses was approaching the end of his life and it was time for someone else to take up the reins.
How was Moses able to help Joshua in this time of transition?

Read John 3:22–30. Imagine the situation with John the Baptist. Many people came to see and hear him; he was certainly a charismatic leader of his time. **In what ways did he relinquish his position, but without giving up his ministry?**

What can you learn and apply from both these situations?

2. Read John 12:23–25. What do you think 'loves his life' means and what are the repercussions? Bearing in mind that 'hate' is used in a different way here from our usual English usage, think through what verses 24 and 25 mean for you. What might you need to give up (or allow to die) in order that more can be achieved? What might you consider to be the 'seeds' that you produce?

3. Read Titus 2:3–5. What does Titus teach us about investing in others?

4. Make a list of people in the Bible who come to your mind who invested in others. Then list the people who were specifically invested in by Jesus in His earthly ministry. Did He limit the type of people He invested in or was He inclusive?

5. The autumn phase of life is about letting go, but not giving up; it is about relinquishing and reinvesting in order to empower others. The time may come for you to give up a major career position, ministry or family responsibility.
Consider how you might use the teaching on this season to help you make a good transition.

6. Think back and reflect on your personal harvest; people you have helped, encouraged or been an inspiration to in your family, church, work and community. Give thanks to God for those opportunities.

 ## Going further

1. Read and consider Psalm 78:1–6. Think about people both from history and in the present day who evidently pass God's teaching on to the next generation. To what extent is this true of you?

2. Read John 15:1–2. In these verses Jesus talks of the need for pruning in order to keep the vine producing fruit. **What sort of spiritual pruning or cutting back do you think might become necessary for you? Do you remember a time when you experienced this? If so, how did it feel at the time and what was the end result?**

Prayer

Thank You, Father, for opportunities to serve You; may my service for You never replace my devotion to You. Help me as I encourage others in their roles, may I be a source of encouragement and help to them as they grow into the people You want them to be. And give me courage, confidence and a spirit of graciousness to recognise when it is time to change.

Into Your hands, Father God, Jesus Christ, Holy Spirit I commit my life, my work, my relationships, myself. Amen.

SESSION 5 –
Extreme Seasons

Extreme seasons

Why are you downcast, O my soul?
Why so disturbed within me?
Put your hope in God,
for I will yet praise him,
my Saviour and my God.

Psalm 42:11

Consider...

Does the thought of extreme seasons excite or worry you?

We have focused on typical British seasonal living for this guide, using seasons as a tool for thinking about spiritual issues. In the same way, Jesus, in His parables, used everyday occurrences to which His listeners related. As I have been completing this chapter, we have just endured the coldest December for one hundred years and a great deal of misery has been caused by the very severe winter conditions. However, many people around the world regularly experience extremes in their climate. The Inuit people live and work in temperatures down to -50°C, whilst others suffer the harshness of drought, floods, violent storms and other such extremes.

In our physical, emotional and spiritual lives we will experience the usual ups and downs, but at some point these normal fluctuations go haywire and we find ourselves feeling very unsettled. We may express this as feeling dried up, burned out, or that we are in the middle of a raging storm; we may talk about God as being silent or even absent. These feelings often accompany a time of personal trauma, particularly if there is a succession of very difficult emotional experiences. It may be of loss – of bereavement, unfaithfulness, health, unemployment or poverty. It may be difficult to work back to the root cause, which may stem from psychological problems such as depression.

In such a short space, it is impossible to do justice to such a big and profoundly impacting topic. It is important not to be superficial, but equally essential not to sweep this under the carpet and avoid it altogether, as it is a season we will probably all face at least once in our lives.

How then may we begin to make any sense of these very difficult times – times which leave us feeling as if we've been overtaken by a tsunami, or left to shrivel to dust under blazing heat? We are going to focus on the theme of suffering as often being the root cause of such seasons of life.

Comforts in the storm and in the desert

One possible comfort is that we are not alone in experiencing suffering. This has been the experience of godly people since the beginning of time, is shared by many of our contemporaries and, no doubt, will continue to be a part of people's lives.

The character of Job in the Old Testament often epitomises deep suffering. He lost his donkeys, oxen and sheep, his camels, his servants, and his sons and daughters. As if his tragic loss were not enough, Job was covered with painful sores. This would be a time when he needed friends to stand alongside and give support, but again Job was let down and instead of bringing comfort they brought their accusations.

I have known people who have done just what Job's 'friends' did, bringing blame rather than comfort. They have suggested that if there had been more faith, more prayer, more devotion, less unbelief, then things would have been different. And so they heap coals on top of the pain already suffered by the suggestion of such guilt. Then these so-called comforters express surprise when the cry goes up – 'Where is God?'

This question forms the heart cry of many of the Psalms. David writes, 'My God, my God, why have you forsaken me? Why are you so far from saving me ...? O my God, I cry out by day, but you do not answer' (Psa. 22:1–2). And again in Psalm 13:1: 'How long, O LORD? Will you forget me for ever? How long will you hide your face from me?' In Psalm 42 we read, 'Why are you downcast, O my soul? Why so disturbed within me? ... I say to God my Rock, "Why have you forgotten me? Why must I go about mourning, oppressed by the enemy?"' (vv.5,9).

Another comfort is that these sufferings do not come from God. God does not punish us for lack of faith, morality or trust. To believe our pain is God's punishment on us is to misunderstand the character of God. For Job, good health and prosperity would be seen as signs of God's blessings. Conversely, sickness and poverty were sure signs of God's displeasure. So there he was, having lived a righteous and God-fearing life, yet seemingly being punished. For him it did not make sense; it flew in the face of all he had believed and built his life on.

So often the question is asked: 'Why should it happen to me, to him, to her – such a wonderful and godly person?' Or, 'Why should such tragedy happen to that family, that organisation, those missionaries who have been such a witness to others?' These questions come from the same source as Job's dilemma – from a belief that suffering is a punishment – so why should God bring such suffering to good people? But Job held on to the sure knowledge that his suffering was not the result of his sin or lack of belief in his God. God is not a capricious God, turning on us when we falter, which is how we sometimes perceive Him when we are less rational. He is on our side!

When I was going through a 'dark tunnel' experience I could not read my Bible or pray in the way I thought most acceptable. I thought of the many people and situations I should be interceding for and felt weighed down with guilt for not praying for them. It was during that time that I walked my dog regularly in a small copse and, as I did so, I let my mind turn to God as Father and to the name of Jesus; always so very precious to me. I could not speak to God as such, or ask anything, but it was just as if I was walking in the company of the Trinity. Those trees became like a cathedral: a special place where I met with God. I began to love those times, and allowed God to be with me without feeling that it was somehow *my task* to communicate with Him and that I was failing. At one time I would have beaten myself up and felt a miserable disappointment to God, but now I could simply accept His acceptance of me. Special as it was, it would not have been good for me to stay in that place forever. I needed to move on when the time was right but I felt, in a tangible way, the utterly unconditional love of God for me and that was something to take with me as I moved on.

Though there are comforts in those difficult places, I believe the great comfort is that God does not want us to remain there: He brings us hope for the future.

In his lovely and thought provoking book, *The One Big Question* (CWR), Michael Baughen writes that there is no thorough solution to the question 'Why?' when it comes to the problems of suffering, but that as Christians we need to know the 'How?': how to prepare for and handle difficult times. The best way of doing this, Baughen suggests, is to go on strengthening the three main pillars of the Christian life: faith, hope and love. I warmly recommend his book to you and we are going to consider these pillars below.

 # Study and discuss

FAITH

Suffering poses a great test to faith, though not for everyone. If our faith is based on the assumption that God will totally keep us from injury or harm, then our faith can be seriously damaged, or even destroyed, very quickly in times of suffering.

1. Read Job 2:10. How did Job answer his wife's mocking?
Despite his friends' suggestion Job maintained his integrity and

righteousness, but he did question God's justice.

2. Read Job 33:8–14. It takes a younger man to effectively challenge Job. What does he bring to Job?
Following this, God Himself speaks to Job in Job 38–41.

3. Read Job 38:1–17. It may also be helpful to skim over chapters 38–41.
What is the gist of what God is saying to Job? What is the particular point made in Job 40:2?

4. Read Habakkuk 3:17–19. Habakkuk expresses deep faith despite his circumstances.
How might you respond to equivalent 21st-century situations?

5. Do you think your faith might be determined by how well life is going for you, or are you able to maintain trust in God in difficult situations?

LOVE

As Christians, we are taught that God is love. Yet my regular experience is that while many women are happy to remind others of God's love, they are not always so quick to accept it for themselves. I wonder why that is. My thoughts are that we live in such a conditional environment that we only feel loved as long as we do, say or are the right thing. And, if we are honest, we also love that way. We love others if they do, say, don't do, or don't say certain things. Paul expresses clearly that God's love is so much beyond such limitations when he talks about how wide, long, high and deep it is.

1. Read Ephesians 3:14–19. Go back and read it again one verse or phrase at a time and savour this prayer of Paul's, written so long ago to the Ephesus church but ringing down the ages to you and me, here and now.
Do you feel fully 'rooted and established in love' (Eph. 3:17) and able to fully accept this for yourself?

2. What difference would it make if we lived in the fullness of God's love when we face difficult circumstances?

3. Does it make a difference if you are with someone who loves you utterly when you are in pain, even though they cannot take that pain away?

HOPE

'There's a light at the end of the tunnel.' How often have you said this, or heard it said? When in the midst of despair, we cling on to the hope that things will get better. If we did not, how would we get through those difficult times?

We often see hope as containing a slight question mark. We hope because we are not certain. However, when we read about hope in God throughout the Bible it has a different feel to it.

1. Read Hebrews 11:1–3. What does this tell us about faith and hope?

2. Read Psalm 25:5; 33:20; 37:9; 42:5; 71:14; Isaiah 40:31 and Jeremiah 29:11. What feel do these verses give for the Hebrew idea of hope in God?

3. Read Matthew 12:21; Acts 23:6; 2 Corinthians 3:11,12; 1 Peter 1:3,13.
How do the New Testament writers understand hope?

Having read these verses, how firm do you consider your hope in God?

Is there anything you would like to take away from these verses for your life?

Wendy Bray is a popular author who has experienced and written about extreme seasons in her life. She writes:

It's natural that in times of darkness and difficulty we will ask 'Why?' But understanding doesn't change what is happening to us. It's likely that instead of saying, 'Well, that makes perfect sense, thank you', we will just pose another question, and another. 'How?' it's true, is a better question, but 'What?' is the boldest and the bravest. 'What can I learn about my character?'; 'What can I do to hear God?'; 'What, in this pain, might transform my relationships?' Yes, I said it was brave. And exhausting. But it is a liberating question to ask in the dark because we can begin to grope around for answers despite our blindness, our fear and our confusion.

When I was very ill with cancer I read – I think the words are Meister Eckhart's – that when we are in a dark place we only know God is there too because He clears His throat in the darkness. That made sense to me: it was surely hard enough to find Him! Later I began to wonder what made Him need to clear His throat. Then I realised: He cries too. He needs to clear His throat because the tears trickle down the back of it. He identifies with my suffering, shares the dark emptiness and weeps alongside me.

When we suffer we understand what it really means to be human. We lose the artificiality that builds our easy assumptions about how life 'should' be and discover that this is how life *is*. We learn, dangerously and painfully, what it really means to trust in an unseen, seemingly incomprehensible God when, really, we want to scream at Him – even as we do. And we can deepen our empathetic compassion and tenderness towards others: the privileged yet costly, unexpected inheritance of many who have suffered.

In dark times all we really need to do is know that we are loved by God and by those we love, and to live in that love. Nothing more is required. No end of answers will fix things for us, no end of questions will make things right through finding understanding. The meaning of suffering – and it surely must have meaning, for God wastes nothing – is a mystery that will only one day be revealed against the vast backdrop of eternity. All we can do, for now, as the wonderful writer and priest Michael Mayne said, is to trust and to love.

Going further

• **Using a concordance or website such as biblegateway.com, make a study of the biblical words faith, hope and love.**

Prayer

I pray for those known to me who are in difficult circumstances; that they will know that You are ever with them and love them. I pray that their faith will be deeply rooted in You and they will understand what it is to know certain hope. May my own faith, hope and knowledge of Your love continue to grow in the good times so they are foundational to my life when the difficult times come. Thank You again for Your immeasurable love.

Into Your hands, Father God, Jesus Christ, Holy Spirit I commit my life, my work, my relationships, myself. Amen.

SESSION 6 –

Rhythms of Grace –
in the light of eternity

Rhythms of Grace – in the light of eternity

There is a time for everything,
and a season for every activity under heaven ...

Ecclesiastes 3:1

Consider...

How have the previous sessions helped you? Do you think you now recognise the various seasons in your life?

We have explored the various seasons, using them to help us understand better the rhythms of our lives and particularly where we are spiritually. Some of these seasons in life are full of frenetic activity, others are marked by a sense of anticipation, and others bringing a period of quiet and rest. Sometimes we get stuck in one season; we might stop so long that we are trapped and cannot find a way forward. We may find ourselves in a season where there is little movement; where we seem to be playing that 'waiting game' forever. Or we might live our lives full on without ever slowing down or taking time to reflect, and then we wonder why we feel so exhausted. In today's jargon – we 'burn out'. Is this how we were intended to live?

Rhythms of grace

As we read about the life of Jesus, we get a feel for living the way God intended. We see those times He spent in preparation, waiting for the right time even before His ministry began. He took time out to rest. He spent extended time alone – such as His time in the desert – and time focusing on the next stage – as on the mount of transfiguration and in the garden of Gethsemane – as He prepared Himself for what was to come. He invested in so many people during His three years of ministry, in particular His disciples but also in countless others including those on, and even beyond, the fringes of society. He was prepared to stand back in order to empower others: He sent His disciples to go out preaching and teaching without Him, and entrusted the news of His resurrection to be taken to the believers, in the first instance by Mary. All this amongst three years of incredible fruitfulness as people flocked to hear and follow Him. Jesus truly embodied what it is to live life effectively in rhythms that were healthy and wholesome.

The way He lived His life gives such force and credibility to His words, so beautifully translated in *The Message*. Read it through slowly a few times and spend time reflecting on it:

'Are you tired? Worn out? Burned out on religion? Come to me. Get away with me and you'll recover your life. I'll show you how to take a real rest. Walk with me and work with me – watch how I do it. Learn the unforced rhythms of grace. I won't lay anything heavy or ill-fitting on you. Keep company with me and you'll learn to live freely and lightly.'

Matthew 11:28–29

What a lovely picture of getting away with Jesus to 'recover my life'. I love the invitation to 'keep company' with Him and that beautiful thought of learning 'the unforced rhythms of grace'. Jesus is inviting us to live our lives with a healthy balance of work and rest, service and being served, as we walk with and learn from Him.

• **Do you go at His pace?**

• **Consider what it means to 'keep company with Him' – to watch how He 'does it'.**

A time and a season for everything

We are reminded of changing seasons in Ecclesiastes 3:1–14:

> *There is a time for everything,*
> *and a season for every activity under heaven:*
> *a time to be born and a time to die,*
> *a time to plant and a time to uproot,*
> *a time to kill and a time to heal,*
> *a time to tear down and a time to build,*
> *a time to weep and a time to laugh,*
> *a time to mourn and a time to dance,*
> *a time to scatter stones and a time to gather them,*
> *a time to embrace and a time to refrain,*
> *a time to search and a time to give up,*
> *a time to keep and a time to throw away,*
> *a time to tear and a time to mend,*
> *a time to be silent and a time to speak,*
> *a time to love and a time to hate,*
> *a time for war and a time for peace.*

> *What does the worker gain from his toil? I have seen the burden God has laid on men. He has made everything beautiful in its time. He has also set eternity in the hearts of men; yet they cannot fathom what God has done from beginning to end. I know that there is nothing better for men than to be happy and do good while they live. That everyone may eat and drink, and find satisfaction in all his toil – this is the gift of God. I know that everything God does will endure for ever; nothing can be added to it and nothing taken from it. God does it, so that men will revere him.*

This sums up much of what we've been looking at. Some of these 'times' are thrust upon us whilst others are chosen, and even those chosen times may be selected consciously or unconsciously. Such constant change can prove to be unsettling and inescapable and can lead to feelings of fatalism, a sense of not being able to do anything about our situations or feeling unable to change them. However, as we look to God and accept God's invitation to walk with Him we can see that whatever our moods, attitudes or circumstances He is with us through them and can bring good out of all of them. We read that, 'He has made everything beautiful in its time' (Eccl. 3:11) and this is a picture of hope we can carry with us.

Eternity

He has also set eternity in the hearts of men; yet they cannot fathom what God has done from beginning to end.
Ecclesiastes 3:11

Within the passage above we read of 'the Teacher' (see Eccl. 1:1) bringing an eternal dimension into his thinking. This constant change which can be so unsettling to the secular world can be seen as an unfolding plan with divine purpose when seen through God's eyes.

The ultimate goal towards which Christians move is eternity with God. We cannot understand all the twists and turns, yet if we are able to recognise and adopt an attitude of aiming for this end result then it can help us to move purposefully towards that goal with confidence that everything is known to the Creator, even if we cannot always make sense of all that happens on the way.

Whatever season of life we find ourselves in, whatever twists and turns are in the road, we can take confidence from the fact that God knows and is walking with us. As we put our lives into His hands we walk with the promise of eternity in our hearts.

Practising patience

I wonder how many of us can simply accept all that happens and wait patiently to know the next step? I guess that will come easily to some, but only a minority. If you are one of those in the minority, please have patience with people like me!

The writers of Scripture knew that to sit and wait with tolerance and without complaint was difficult for most people. That is why they so often reminded their original readers of the importance of patience. And nothing seems to have changed on that score. James writes:

> *Be patient, then, brothers, until the Lord's coming. See how the farmer waits for the land to yield its valuable crop and how patient he is for the autumn and spring rains.*
>
> *James 5:7*

It is not helpful for the farmer to keep digging up his seeds to see how they are doing underground, and equally there is no point in harvesting the crop until it is fully ripened. He must wait patiently for the right time. How often do we want to rush on to the next stage when God has more to do with us at our present stage?

• Do you find it hard waiting for God's purposes to unfold in your life? If so, how can you change and learn to wait patiently and trustingly?

The passage in James 5 from which this verse is taken goes on to encourage patience in the face of suffering. It is natural to want suffering to be over, yet even in that place we are encouraged to persevere in the way that the prophets of the Old Testament did.

 ## Study and discuss:

For this section there are only a few suggested tasks, but they can take as much time as you are willing to give them.

1. Take the phrases from Ecclesiastes 3:2–8 and write in your own experiences underneath them:

For example, alongside 'a time to mourn ...' write something about a time when you mourned. Some of the questions you may like to reflect on as you do this are: how did that time of mourning arise? How did it feel? How did it affect you and others? How did you respond? What was the short-term and then longer-term impact on you? Ask the same questions about a time you danced – whether literally, metaphorically or both. If studying as a group you could split the phrases between different people.

- a time to be born and a time to die,
  a time to plant and a time to uproot,

- a time to kill and a time to heal,
  a time to tear down and a time to build,

- a time to weep and a time to laugh,
  a time to mourn and a time to dance,

- a time to scatter stones and a time to gather them,
  a time to embrace and a time to refrain,

- a time to search and a time to give up,
  a time to keep and a time to throw away,

- a time to tear and a time to mend,
  a time to be silent and a time to speak,

- a time to love and a time to hate,
  a time for war and a time for peace.

2. Do you need encouragement to be patient with your present situation?

3. Ponder on the phrase, 'He has made everything beautiful in its time' (Eccl. 3:11). What do you think this means? What do you think and feel as you contemplate what this means for you personally?

4. How has the goal of eternity helped you in the past? How might it help you in your present and in the future?

And finally …

As we start to unpack these seasons, remember again that they are not about age or about the time of year. They are about learning to discern God's rhythms in our lives so that we move at His pace, not always wanting to be somewhere else, but discerning what it is that God wants of us at this time.

Prayer

Into Your hands, Father God, Jesus Christ, Holy Spirit I commit my life, my work, my relationships, myself. Amen.

I suggest you take each of the questions below and use your answers as a basis for your personal prayer as we come to the end of this study.

Where am I in relation to God at this time?
What is it that God wants of me at this time?
How can I make the most of this stage?
How might I be better prepared for what is to come?
How can I celebrate the seasons in my life?

As we learn to live and work with God, as we keep company with Him, as we walk with Him ever more closely, so we learn how to live more in harmony with those seasons that He brings into our lives.

Where can women find security in this insecure world?

Drawing on examples of women in the Bible and women today you will learn practical steps leading to the lasting security found only in a relationship with God.

Eight sessions for individual or group use.

How to be a Secure Woman
by Jeannette Barwick and Catherine Butcher
96-page boolet, 148x210mm
ISBN: 978-1-85345-307-6

Understand yourself and others better

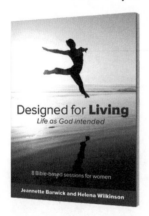

Discover God's original design for your life with this eight-session resource for women. Explore your deepest longings, motives and patterns of thinking and relating, and find security and personal significance as you learn to draw more thoroughly on the Father's love for you.

Suitable for group or individual use.

Designed for Living workbook
by Jeannette Barwick and Helena Wilkinson
96-page booklet, 148x210mm
ISBN: 978-1-85345-523-0

For current prices visit www.cwr.org.uk/store

Available online or from Christian bookshops.